Fun Riddles

&

Trick Questions

For Kids and Family

300 Riddles and Brain Teasers
That
Kids and Family Will Enjoy!

Riddleland

Table of Contents

Introduction

"Play is our brain's favorite way to learn" - Diane Ackerman

We would like to personally thank you for purchasing this book. **Fun Riddles and Trick Questions for Kids and Family!** is a collection of 300 fun brain teasers and riddles of easy to hard difficulty.

These brain teasers will challenge children and their parents to think and stretch their minds. They also have many other benefits, such as:

• **Bonding** – It is an excellent way for parents and their children to spend some quality time and create some fun and memorable memories.

• **Confidence Building** - When parents give the riddles, it creates a safe environment for children to burst out with the answers even if they are incorrect. This helps children to develop self-confidence in expressing themselves.

- **Improve Vocabulary** – Riddles are usually written in advanced words; therefore, children will need to understand these words before they can share the riddles.

- **Better reading comprehension** – Many children can read at a young age but may not understand the context of the words. Riddles can help develop the children's interest to comprehend the context before they can share them with their friends.

- **Sense of humor** – Funny creative riddles can help children develop their sense of humor while getting their brains working.

Bonus Book!

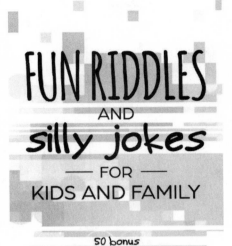

RIDDLELAND

http://bit.ly/Riddelandbonus

Thank you for buying this book. We would like to share a special bonus as a token of appreciation. It is a collection of 50 original jokes, riddles, and two funny stories

Chapter 1: Easy Riddles

"Play gives children a chance to practice what they are learning" – Mr. Rogers

1. Cheese backward

What cheese is made backward?

2. Short and tall

I'm short when I'm old, but tall when I'm young. What am I?

3. Word with Letter E

This word begins and ends with an E but contains only one letter. What is it?

4. Hands that can't clap

What has hands but cannot clap?

5. Up vs. Down

What goes up but never goes down?

6. Filled with Ts

This starts with a T, ends with a T, and is filled with tea - what is it?

7. End of the rainbow

What do you find at the end of a rainbow?

8. Wet vs. dry

What gets wetter the more that it dries?

9. Months and days

There are seven months with 31 days, but which of the months have 28 days?

10. Rocks or feathers

Which object weighs more: a pound of rocks or a pound of feathers?

11. Appearing in

What appears once in a minute, twice in a moment, and not once in a thousand years?

12. Seconds in a year

How many seconds are found in a year?

13. Tires on a street

You're driving around in a fancy car. Which of your tires don't move when you turn right onto a street?

14. Served but not eaten

What is served but is never eaten?

15. It grows bigger

The more you remove from it, the bigger it grows. What is it?

16. They all have...

What do a shark, a comb, and a zipper all have in common?

17. Birthdays are good for you

How do you know that birthdays are good for you?

18. Five fingers

I am not alive, but I have five fingers. What am I?

19. Tigers vs. comedians

Why don't tigers eat comedians?

20. Funny Bone

What cannot laugh but still has a funny bone?

21. Around the world

What can travel the whole way around the world while staying in the very same corner?

22. Sound likes bacon frying

I can move quickly, but I have no legs. My skin will shed when I grow bigger. I can sound like bacon frying. What am I?

23. Feed me

Give me a drink, and I will die but feed me, and I will grow bigger. What am I?

24. No matter how hard it rains

What never gets any wetter than it is today, no matter how hard it rains?

25. 100 feet in the air

My back is on the ground, but my 100 feet are in the air. What am I?

26. Hot in the refrigerator

What is always hot, even if you store it in a refrigerator?

27. Cracked!

I can be made or cracked or played. I can be bad or dad or funny. What am I?

28. Fish, Music, and bathroom

What can you find on a fish, in music, or under your bathroom sink?

29. Baby chick

When is the best time to buy a baby chick?

30. Mt Everest

Mt. Everest was discovered in 1856. Before it was discovered, what was the highest mountain on Earth?

31. Stolen Feathers

What flies through the air on stolen feathers?

32. Red and Green

When is it OK to go on red and stop at green?

33. Leaves with spine

What has leaves, but no branches? A spine, but no bones?

34. Four seasons

Summer is here, so I'm wearing green. When fall comes, I change into yellow. When winter comes, I'll get rid of my covers. What am I?

35. Food that sounds like I do

What food sounds like I do when I see a ghost?

36. Animals and creatures

Most animals and creatures grow up, but which creatures grow down?

37. Ears that can't hear

What is all ears, but doesn't hear a single thing you say?

38. Falls vs. breaks

What falls but never breaks - and what breaks but never falls?

39. Holes that holds water

What has a lot of holes but can still hold water?

40. T island

How is an island like the letter "T"?

41. Favorite drink in the south

I am the favorite drink in England. With just three letters in my name, I can lose the last two and still sound the same. What am I?

42. Turtles and chicken nuggets

Why don't turtles go through the drive-thru for chicken nuggets?

43. Up and down

What never moves, but often goes up and down?

44. Nut with a hole

Which nut has a hole?

45. Sound of my house

If you can hear the sound of my house, I am no longer there. What am I?

46. Without a head

What has a bottom and a neck, but no head?

47. A cup that we can't drink

What type of cup can you never take a drink from?

48. Last daughter's name

Hannah's mother has four daughters. One is called Becky; one is Ann, and one is called Susie. What is the name of the last daughter?

49. Creature in the ocean

What is the strongest creature in the ocean?

50. Being with a fool

What is even more dangerous than being with a fool?

51. Novel into a stream

How can you turn a novel into a stream?

52. Running through the U.S with five eyes

What runs through the U.S. and has five eyes?

53. Soccer, football, and baseball

What happens once in soccer, twice in football, but never in baseball?

54. Bad luck black cat

When is it bad luck for a black cat to cross your path?

55. Cat burglar

How do you know if a cat burglar has broken into your house?

56. Pie crust and the dentist

Why did the pie crust visit the dentist?

57. Nobody wants it

The person who makes it doesn't use it; the owner doesn't want it, and the user has no idea they are using it. What is it?

58. Four families in a house

Four families live together in one house. When separated, the families contain two reds and two blacks. What are we?

59. Terrible dancers

Why are elephants terrible dancers?

60. Talking donkey

What is smarter than a talking donkey?

61. Still dead

What isn't alive, but can still be dead?

62. Cat, dog, and school

A cat has three, a dog has three, but a school has six. What is it?

63. When the rain comes down

What goes up when the rain comes down?

64. Without sleep

A man in London did not sleep one single day for a whole year. How did he survive?

65. Hot or Cold

Which travels faster, hot or cold?

66. Without touching

What can you hold without ever touching it with your hands?

67. Frog jump

What kind of frog can jump higher than a building?

68. No doors or windows

What kind of room doesn't have any windows or doors?

69. Rip and scratch

Rip one-off and scratch the head; what was red is now black instead. What is it?

70. Peeling my skin

If you peel off my skin, I won't even cry. But I think you will. What am I?

71. Can't See

What has only one eye but still can't see?

72. Catch but can't throw

What can you catch, but you cannot throw?

73. Never gets here

What is always coming but can never get here?

74. Dog Catcher

When a dog catcher catches 20 dogs in a week, how does he get paid?

75. Broken

What gets broken if it isn't kept?

76. Frequently Answered

What is frequently answered even though it has never asked a question?

77. What does she weigh?

Susan is a butcher. She is five feet, five inches, and wears size six shoes. What does she weigh?

78. 4th of July

Do they have a 4th of July in Spain?

79. Lock that can't open

What two keys cannot open a lock?

80. Most stories

What building has the most stories?

81. Chicken and Egg

A farmer has 12 chickens, and all but eight die. How many are still laying eggs?

82. Hand Tree

What kind of tree can you carry in your hand?

83. Only a tail and head

What has a tail and a head but does not have a body?

84. Birthdays

How many birthdays does the average kid have?

85. A wet coat

What type of coat do you only put on when it is wet?

86. Can't have for lunch

What are the only two things you can't have for lunch?

87. Alphabet

How many letters are there in the alphabet?

88. Light as feather

I am as light as a feather, but the biggest, strongest person cannot hold me for 10 minutes.

89. More and less

The more there is of me, the less you see. What am I?

90. Doubling money

What is the fastest and easiest way to double your money?

91. Cities without anything

This has cities without people, beaches without sand, oceans with no water, and mountains with no peaks. What is it?

92. Without moving

I have gone through towns, cities, and hills, but have never moved. How can that be?

93. Has a mouth

What never walks but always runs; never talks but can murmur; never sleeps, but has a bed; never eats, but has a mouth?

94. Never open any door

This is full of keys but can never open any door. What is it?

95. Biggest Ant

What is the biggest ant that lives in storybooks?

96. Queen

What is above the queen?

97. Hard to throw

What is easy to lift but difficult to throw?

98. What am I?

I have a little house where I live. In my house, there aren't any doors or windows. If I want to leave, I must break through a wall. What am I?

99. Leave it behind

Everyone has one, but they always leave it behind. What is it?

100. Won't fit the biggest pot

This won't fit in the biggest pot in the kitchen. What is it?

101. Every direction

What can point in every direction but cannot reach any destination by itself?

102. Plane survivors

A 747 is flying from California to Chicago and crashes on the border of Utah and Colorado. Where will they bury the survivors?

103. Forward and backward

Forward I am very heavy, but when backward, I am not. What am I?

104. Winter and Summer

This lives in winter, dies in the summer, and grows its roots upward. What is it?

105. Others will use it more often

It may belong to you, but others will use it more often than you do. What is it?

106. Flying without wings

What flies without wings; can cry but doesn't have eyes?

107. Artificial leg

In Philadelphia, you can't take a picture of a man with an artificial leg. Why not?

108. Always talk back

What cannot speak, but will always talk back when spoken to?

109. Christmas before Thanksgiving

When does Christmas come before Thanksgiving?

110. Taste vs. smell

What tastes much better than it smells?

111. Only light

In a place with light is the only place I can survive, but if light shines right on me, I die. What am I?

112. Under the sun

What can pass under the sun without ever casting a shadow?

113. Amount of dirt

How much dirt is there in a hole that is 4 feet wide and 5 feet deep?

114. Stamps

How many six-cent stamps are in two dozen?

115. Shaving a beard

Several times a day, I shave, but my beard is long and full. How can that be?

116. Everything or nothing

If you turn me on my side, then I am everything forever. But if you cut me in half, then I become nothing.

117. Rooster laying eggs

If a rooster lays a white egg and a brown egg, what sort of babies will hatch from each egg?

118. Disappear and reappear

I will travel from there to here by disappearing here and reappearing there. What am I?

119. Green House

If a brown house is made of brown wood, and a red house is made of red bricks, then what is a greenhouse made of?

120. 10 Wheels

Which type of transportation has ten wheels, but can only carry one person?

121. Always answer

I never ask you a question, but you will answer me. Why?

122. Right-hand advice

What kind of advice can you get from your right hand?

123. Can't walk or stand

What has a back and four legs, but cannot stand or walk?

124. Buried up to my neck

I am buried up to my neck in work. You can pat me on the top of the head when I hold it all together. What am I?

125. Studying on the airplane

Why did the kid study on the airplane?

126. Sun and college

Why didn't the sun go to college?

127. King of the Classroom

Who is the king of the classroom?

128. Computer and Lunch

What did the computer do for lunch?

129. Favorite Dessert

What is the math teacher's favorite dessert?

130. Hundred dollar note

Is an old one-hundred-dollar note more valuable than a new one?

131. Never Eaten

What is put on a table to be cut, but never eaten?

132. Never eat me

You go to the store and buy me to eat, but then never eat me. Why not?

133. Break easily

You cannot see me or touch me, but you can break me easily. What am I?

134. Without a head

I am higher without a head than I am with it. What am I?

135. Can't walk or hug

It has 50 limbs but cannot walk or hug you. What is it?

136. Eye that is blind

What has an eye but cannot see?

137. Like a stone

I am hard like a stone, but I grow on your body. What am I?

138. An unbuttoned button

What kind of a button cannot be unbuttoned?

139. Timid lion

What kind of lion never roars?

140. Rings without fingers

What has many rings, but no fingers?

Chapter 2: Easy Riddle Answers

1. **Answer**: Edam. Edam is a semi-hard cheese from the Netherlands

2. **Answer**: A Candle

3. **Answer**: An Envelope

4. **Answer**: The long and shorthand on the face of a clock

5. **Answer**: Your Age

6. **Answer**: A Teapot

7. **Answer**: The letter W

8. **Answer**: A towel

9. **Answer**: All of them

10. **Answer**: Neither, both of them weigh a pound

11. **Answer**: The letter M

12. **Answer**: 12: January 2nd, February 2nd, March 2nd, April 2nd, (get it)

13. **Answer**: Your spare tire

14. **Answer**: A volleyball

15. **Answer**: A hole

16. **Answer**: They all have teeth

17. **Answer**: The more birthdays you have, the longer you live

18. **Answer**: A glove

19. **Answer**: They taste funny

20. **Answer**: A skeleton

21. **Answer**: A postage stamp

22. **Answer**: A snake

23. **Answer**: Fire

24. **Answer**: The ocean or lake

25. **Answer**: A centipede lying on its back on the ground, with all 100 feet waving in the air.

26. **Answer**: Tabasco or chili sauce

27. **Answer**: A joke

28. **Answer**: Scales

29. **Answer**: when they are going cheap (cheep – cheep)

30. **Answer**: Still Mt Everest

31. **Answer**: An arrow (or dart)

32. **Answer**: When you're eating a watermelon

33. **Answer**: A Book

34. **Answer**: A tree (with leaves)

35. **Answer**: Ice cream (I scream)

36. **Answer**: A Geese (Down feathers)

37. **Answer**: A field of corn

38. **Answer**: Night and day

39. **Answer**: A sponge

40. **Answer**: It's in the middle of the water

41. **Answer**: Tea

42. **Answer**: They don't like fast food

43. **Answer**: The temperature

44. **Answer**: A doughnut

45. **Answer**: A seashell (if you hold it to your ear, you can hear the ocean; but if you are holding the shell to your ear, it isn't in the ocean anymore)

46. **Answer**: A bottle

47. **Answer**: A hiccup

48. **Answer**: Hannah, it said so in the beginning

49. **Answer**: The mussel

50. **Answer**: Fooling with a bee

51. **Answer**: Turn "book" into "brook"

52. **Answer**: The Mississippi River

53. **Answer**: The letter "O."

54. **Answer**: When you're a mouse

55. **Answer**: Your cat is missing

56. **Answer**: Because it needed filling

57. **Answer**: A coffin

58. **Answer**: A deck of cards

59. **Answer**: Because they have two left feet

60. **Answer**: A spelling bee

61. **Answer**: An AA battery

62. **Answer**: Letters

63. **Answer**: An umbrella

64. **Answer**: He slept at night

65. **Answer**: Hot, because everyone catches a cold

66. **Answer**: Your breath

67. **Answer**: Any frog because buildings can't jump

68. **Answer**: A mushroom

69. **Answer**: Matchstick

70. **Answer**: An onion

71. **Answer**: A needle

72. **Answer**: The common cold

73. **Answer**: Tomorrow

74. **Answer**: By the pound

75. **Answer**: A promise

76. **Answer**: A doorbell

77. **Answer**: Meat

78. **Answer**: Yes, but they do not celebrate it as Independence Day

79. **Answer**: A donkey or a monkey

80. **Answer**: A library

81. **Answer**: 8

82. **Answer**: A palm (tree)

83. **Answer**: A coin

84. **Answer**: Just one – we all have just one

85. **Answer**: A coat of paint

86. **Answer**: breakfast and dinner

87. **Answer**: 11 letters are in "the alphabet."

88. **Answer**: Breath

89. **Answer**: Darkness

90. **Answer**: Hold it in front of a mirror

91. **Answer**: A map

92. **Answer**: I am a road

93. **Answer**: A river

94. **Answer**: A piano

95. **Answer**: A gi-ant

96. **Answer**: Her crown

97. **Answer**: A feather

98. **Answer**: A baby chick in its egg

99. **Answer**: A fingerprint

100. **Answer**: The lid

101. **Answer**: A compass

102. **Answer**: The survivors are still alive.

103. **Answer**: Ton

104. **Answer**: An Icicle

105. **Answer**: Your name

106. **Answer**: A cloud

107. **Answer**: You have to use a camera

108. **Answer**: An echo

109. **Answer**: In the dictionary

110. **Answer**: Your tongue

111. **Answer**: A shadow

112. **Answer**: A gust of wind

113. **Answer**: There is no dirt in a hole

114. **Answer**: 24, there are always 24 in two dozen

115. **Answer**: I am a barber

116. **Answer**: The number 8. On its side, it looks like an infinity symbol; if you cut it in half then it looks like two zeros

117. **Answer**: Rooster don't lay eggs, hens do.

118. **Answer**: The letter "T."

119. **Answer**: Glass (it lets in the most light to grow flowers)

120. **Answer**: Inline skates

121. **Answer**: Telephone

122. **Answer**: Finger "Tips"

123. **Answer**: A Chair

124. **Answer**: A nail

125. **Answer**: He wanted a higher education

126. **Answer**: Because it already had a million degrees

127. **Answer**: The ruler

128. **Answer**: He had a byte

129. **Answer**: Pi

130. **Answer**: Yes, $100 is always worth more than $1

131. **Answer**: A deck of cards

132. **Answer**: Because it is a plate

133. **Answer**: A promise

134. **Answer**: A pillow

135. **Answer**: A tree

136. **Answer**: A tornado

137. **Answer**: A tooth

138. **Answer**: A belly button

139. **Answer**: A dande-lion

140. **Answer**: A telephone

Chapter 3: Hard Riddles

"The field of creativity that exists within each individual is freed by moving out of ideas of wrongdoing or right doing." – Angles Arrien

1. Three Monkeys

You are in a room with three monkeys: one has a stick, one has a banana, and one has nothing. Who is the smartest primate?

2. Yesterday and Tomorrow

I am where yesterday is after today, but tomorrow is in the middle. Where would I be?

3. Crossing the river

A boy stands on one bank of the river, and his dog, Bullet, stands on the other bank. The boy calls his dog, who crosses the river to get to him. Bullet doesn't use a bridge and doesn't get wet. How is it possible?

4. Measure but can't see

What can be measured but cannot actually be seen?

5. 21st Birthday

A man was born in 2001 and today is his 21st birthday. How is this possible?

6. Turn once and again

If I turn once, what is out will get in. But if I turn around again, what is in will not get out. What am I?

7. Foot and Yard

What is worn by the foot but bought by the yard?

8. Man with a mustache

A man with a mustache pushes his race car to a property with a hotel and tells the owner of the hotel he is bankrupt. Why would he do that?

9. Lots of House

There was a big greenhouse. Inside that greenhouse was a smaller white house. Inside the white house, there was a smaller red house. And inside the red house, there were a lot of little ones ready to grow. What am I?

10. Combining letters

What two words, when combined together, have the most letters?

11. Dropping me

If you drop me in water, I will die. But if you drop me from the tallest building, I will be just fine.

12. Thirteen Hearts

What has thirteen hearts, but doesn't have any other organs?

13. Unpopular Vegetable

What type of vegetable is unpopular on pirate ships?

14. Outdoor Sport

Which sport, played outside around the world, has four letters and begins with a "T"?

15. Full of holes

I am the most useful when I am full, but yet I am always full of holes. What am I?

16. Never moves

What goes both down and up but never moves?

17. Twins, Queen and King

Two twins, a queen, and a king are all inside a big room. But there aren't any adults in the room. How is that possible?

18. Moving pieces

A sundial has the least amount of moving parts of any device that tells time. Which timepiece has the most moving pieces?

19. Work makes me thin

The more I work, the thinner I get. What am I?

20. Loses in the morning

What loses its head first thing in the morning and gets it back the last thing at night?

21. Not enough room

You have a key and can enter, but cannot come in. I have space, but not enough room. What am I?

22. Unique number

What is unique about the number 8,549,176,320?

23. Cold bear hot

What one letter can you change to make a cold polar bear hot?

24. Longest river

Historically, before the Amazon River was discovered, what was the longest river in the world?

25. White Items

Which one of these actually isn't white: golf ball, polar bear, milk, marshmallow, egg white, the White House, or white onions?

26. Changing colors

If you paint a white house green, it will become a green house. If you color the picture of a banana it is yellow. If you throw a white scarf into the Red Sea, what will it become?

27. Improving your day

I cannot be seen, I cannot be touched, you won't hear me, and you can't feel me. But I can improve your day - what am I?

28. Rubber Ducks

Four rubber ducks are floating in a tub with Ashley; 2 fall out of the tub on the floor; 2 sink to the bottom and drown. How many ducks are still alive?

29. Smartest State

What is the smartest U.S. state?

30. Stopping dolphins from being extinct

What do dolphins have that no other creature has that keeps them from going extinct?

31. Jack of all trades

I am a person, a bird, and a fruit; what am I?

32. Fishermen and Instrument

I am what fishermen do or maybe a Spanish instrument. What am I?

33. Where are the cookies?

It was Christmas morning in Boston when Mom had to go to the store for more milk. The youngest daughter was watching Dora the Explorer. The middle daughter was reading a book. The oldest son was mowing the front yard. Dad was watching the news. When Mom came home, all the cookies were gone, who ate them?

34. Can't answer a question

What question can you never answer "yes" to?

35. Needed by the President and the kid

I can be high or low; I can run fast or slow. I am needed by both the President and the kid down the street. What am I?

36. Birthday in summer

Why did a woman born in December celebrate her birthday in summer?

37. Popular around the world

Several times a day, people from all over the world visit me. Some may think I'm dirty, even on my best day, but no one wants to live without me. What am I?

38. Insect name

I'm an insect and the first part of my name is a different insect too. What am I?

39. Jump and stand

I jump when I'm walking and stand when I'm sitting. What am I?

40. Ancient Invention

What is the ancient invention that allows people to see through walls?

41. Ancient Roar

Old and ancient, it runs for centuries but never moves. It has a mighty roar, but no lungs or throat. What is it?

42. Eggs in a basket

There are seven people at a farm picking eggs. There are seven eggs in the basket and each person gets to take one egg. When they each take an egg, there is still one egg left in the basket, how is that possible?

43. No escape

I have keys and also some locks; I have space but not an empty room. You can enter but cannot exit. What am I?

44. Multiple eyes and faces

I have twenty-one eyes and six faces. But I cannot see and you can't touch my cheeks. What am I?

45. Dozens of letter

What seven-letter word can have dozens of letters?

46. Parrot and Orange

What sounds like a parrot and is orange?

47. Sharing

If you have me, you really want to share me. But if you share me, then you don't have me. What am I?

48. Help you see

What has two arms, but no hands. No eyes, but can help you see?

49. Butterfly legs

How many legs does a butterfly have if you call the antennae legs?

50. Start with letter T

Which 4 days of the week begin with the letter "T"?

51. Black, Red, and Grey

It is black when you buy it, red when you use it, and grey when you throw it away. What is it?

52. Branches without limbs

What has a lot of branches but no limbs or leaves?

53. Higher than an elephant

Which animal can jump higher than an elephant?

54. Making it lighter

You have a small blue bucket filled to the top with sand from the beach. It is very heavy, so what can you add to the bucket that will make it easier to carry and lighter?

55. Feet without legs

What has feet but doesn't have legs?

56. Scientist and Helium

Did you hear the riddle about the scientist who was reading a textbook on Helium?

57. Not twins

A mother had two daughters who were born in the same year, on the same day, and even on the same hour. But they were not twins. How?

58. Looking for something

Whenever you lose something, you find it in the very last place you look, why is that?

59. Camping

You're camping and have a match, a candle, an oil lamp, and a campfire. When it gets dark, which one do you light first?

60. Poke Me in the Eye

You might have to poke me in the eye for me to do what I'm supposed to do. Sometimes I live in a box or I can sit on a cushion. One place you rarely find me is in a haystack. What am I?

61. Pony eating hay

A pony is tied to a 20-foot rope and there is a bale of hay 25-feet away from her. The pony is still able to eat the hay, how is that possible?

62. Many doors

You are in a maze, trying to escape. There are three doors leading out of the maze. A sign at each door tells you what is inside. Door #1 is a lava pool. Door #2 is a group of ninjas. Door 3 is a scary lion that hasn't eaten in 4 months. Which door should you pick?

63. Three blind mice

Where did the three blind mice moor their boats?

64. House rules

You are in Rebecca's house and there is one rule that cannot be broken. You can have pizza but cannot have a burger. You can use pepper but cannot use salt. You can leave by the door, but it isn't an exit. What is the rule?

65. Favorite subject

What is a snake's favorite subject in school?

66. Two heads and tails

What has two tails, two heads, and walks around on four legs?

67. Everything green

In a one-story greenhouse, there was a green alien, a green fish, a green lizard, a green book, a green table, a green computer, a green rug - you get it, everything was green! What color are the stairs?

68. Without an umbrella

An old man was walking in the park and it started raining. The man wasn't wearing a hat and didn't have an umbrella. His jacket was soaking wet, but not a hair on his head got wet. How is this possible?

69. With and without me

I am at the beginning of sadness and the end of sickness. You cannot have any happiness without me, yet I am part of sacrifice. I am never in danger but always within risk. Never out of darkness, but not in the light.

70. Sheriff in town

A sheriff in the old west rides into town on a Friday; he stays for three days in town and leaves on Friday. How is this possible?

71. Throwing a ball

I threw a ball as hard as I could, and it came right back to me even though I hadn't bounced it off of anything - how is this possible?

72. Falling off a ladder

Johnny was fixing the roof and fell off a 20-foot ladder. Yet he didn't get hurt. Why not?

73. High-Speed Train

If a high-speed electric train in Japan is going west at 100 mph and there is a strong wind to the north, which way does the smoke from the smokestack float?

74. Circus in town

You own a circus and are moving to a new town for your next show. Your lions all weigh about 400 pounds each. How many male lions can you put in an empty truck that can carry two tons?

75. Letters

Give away my first letter, take my second letter. Then take away all the rest of my letters. I will remain the same. What am I?

76. Favorite food

What is a frog's favorite food?

77. What am I eating?

When I was eating my picnic item, I threw away the outside and cooked the inside. And then I ate the outside and threw away the inside. What was I eating?

78. Manholes

You are walking down the streets of New York City and notice the manhole covers are all round. Why is that?

79. Subtracting letters

I have six letters but subtract the last one and I will have twelve.

80. Touching the sky

I can touch the sky. I can touch the Earth. But if I touch you, you will be shocked. What am I?

81. Curvy and straight

I come in all shapes and sizes. I am curvy but am also straight. You can place me wherever you like, but there is only one place I belong to. What am I?

82. Fun in snow

When I am full, you may see me wave. But when I am empty, I can't move a thing. I'm in the middle of the fun in the snow, but I'm hidden away on a sunny day. What am I?

83. Eggs

Which one is the correct sentence: "the yolk of the egg is white" or "the yolk of the egg are white?"

84. Fresh vegetable

What type of vegetable is only sold fresh - never frozen, canned, in jars, or pickled?

85. Counting apples

If you have four apples in your left hand and five in your right, what do you have?

86. Hot food

What food gets hotter when it sounds colder?

87. Dropping an egg

Can you drop a raw egg on a cement floor without cracking it?

88. White and round

I'm white and round but sometimes I cannot be found. At sunny noon, you won't see my face. What am I?

89. Fruits in a bowl

There's a fruit bowl on Grandma's table containing two types of fruit. If you jumble the letters of one, you can spell the other. What are the two fruits?

90. Still some left

If I can take away the whole and still have some left, what am I thinking about?

91. It's snowing

Bess wakes up on a bright morning and without even opening her eyes, knows it had been snowing. How?

92. Something in common

What can be found on a potato or in a hurricane or on the farmer who grows the first and is afraid of the second?

93. Going the wrong way

A police officer is sitting in his police car when he notices a truck driver going the wrong way down a one-way street. The police officer does not arrest the driver, or even stop him. Why not?

94. What doesn't belong?

Which one doesn't belong: egg, banana, apple, walnut, tangerine, or avocado?

95. Cooking eggs

How is your maths? If it takes 11 minutes to hard-boil an egg, how long does it take to hard-boil 272 eggs?

96. Something tiny

A carpenter was building a bookshelf when a tiny thing stopped him. He didn't want it and tried to get rid of it. But he couldn't find it, so he took it home with him. What stopped him?

97. Colored balls

There is a mix of blue, yellow, and red balls in a box. The total o number of balls is 60. There are four times as many yellow balls as there are red balls and six more blue balls than red balls. How many balls of each color ball are there?

98. Ordering pizza

Two fathers and two sons went out for dinner. They each wanted a whole pizza for themselves. When the waiter comes, they ordered three pizzas - why?

99. Hidden identity

A woman goes into a coffee shop and orders lunch. She ate a sandwich, a slice of pie, and drank a can of soda. How does the waitress know that she is a policewoman?

100. Subtracting numbers

How many times can you subtract 5 from 25?

101. Boy scout

Tom is a boy scout and has his monthly inspection tomorrow. Unfortunately, when working on his art project, he had blue ink on his finger. It won't come off with soap, but his Mum hides it for his meeting. How?

102. Baseball games

You are attending a baseball game with your dad. The Bluebirds won the game with a score of 12 to 8. There were no errors, but not a single man crossed the plate. How did that happen?

103. Farmer and his crows

A farmer sees 10 crows on his scarecrow on the edge of the cornfield. He shoots at one. How many crows remain??

104. Practicing for the Olympics

Beth is practicing for the Olympics. She jumps 150 feet all on her own. She lands safely and makes the team. How did she do it?

105. Cows and people drink it

Cows drink it and every morning, lots of people have it in their coffee. What is it?

106. Stuck on an Island

A man was trapped on a small desert island in the center of a big lake. The man couldn't swim and didn't have a boat or a cell phone. He waited and hoped for someone to save him, but no one came. A few months later, he got off the island. How?

107. Stopping the fight

Bob and Tom get in trouble with their Mum for fighting. She takes out a newspaper and makes them both stand on a sheet of the newspaper without speaking until they were ready to make peace. To make sure they didn't touch and continue the fight, how did she place the boys?

108. Words that rhyme

Sunday dinner is a roast. We take our holiday on the coast. What do you put in a toaster?

109. Letter plays

With three letters, I am "consume." With four, I am on fire. With just one more, I can be what you are consuming when it's hot. What am I?

110. Photoshoot in Africa

Barbara is a photographer on a photoshoot in Africa. As she is taking a picture of a lion, she puts her hand in her pocket to find something in there with a tail and a head. But she doesn't scream and isn't afraid. Why not?

111. Prickly and sweet

I am not a queen but have a crown. I can be both prickly and sweet. What am I?

112. Hair cut

A barber in Philadelphia comments that he would rather cut the hair of three men from New Jersey than just one man from Philadelphia. Why would he make that kind of comment?

113. Sailors on a ship

Two sailors are on the deck of a ship on opposite sides. One looks east while the other looks west. But both can see the other. How is that possible?

114. Super useful

I can be used to build castles, help one man to see, but make the next one blind. What am I?

115. Label

Yesterday, I was running late for school and I got dressed really fast in the dark. When I put on my t-shirt, I had it on inside-out with my right arm in the left sleeve and my left arm in the right sleeve. Where can you see my label?

116. Science teacher

Your science teacher, Mrs. Winters, has three favorite states, what are they?

117. Colorful

There are three parts of me, but when you say me out loud, I sound like only one. I can be found in pairs or alone. For some, I am green, others I'm brown, and can even be black and blue. What am I?

118. Librarian contest

The librarian of your school announces a new contest. She says that a $50 note is to be found between pages 75 and 76 of her favorite book. Your best friend runs off to find it, but you did not move. Why not?

119. Chances

Mrs. Whitcomb has three children, the oldest is a boy, the second is a boy, what are the chances that the third child will be a boy?

120. Spelling

Train Crossing: Beware of Cars! Can you spell that without any Rs?

121. Related Presidents

The 24th and the 22nd U.S. President were related, have the same parents, but were not brothers. How is that possible?

122. Spelling

Can you rearrange the letters in NEW DOOR to spell one word?

123. Differences

What is the difference between a jailer and a jeweler?

124. Mother and daughter

The ages of a mother and daughter add up to 66. The mother's age is the daughter's age is reversed. How old are the pair?

125. Letter play

Remove my first letter, I'll still sound the same. Remove my last letter, I'll still sound the same. You can even remove the letter in my middle, and I'll sound the same. I'm a five-letter word – which one?

126. Type of wood

I was traveling to town and met a man on a bridge with a load of wood. The wood was neither crooked or straight and the man was not struggling under the weight. What kind of wood was it?

127. White car

If everyone in the country bought a white vehicle, what would we have?

128. Four men

Four men meet: the first is a master of love, the second a commander of shovels, the third a master of mastery, and the last a leader of priceless gems. Who are they?

129. Who paid the bill?

Friday, Max, and Jason met at a diner for lunch. After eating, they paid the bill. But neither Max nor Jason paid, so who did?

130. Pronunciation

If you pronounce me correctly, it will be wrong. If you pronounce me wrong, it will be correct. What word am I?

131. What am I?

I have neither eyes nor ears nor a tongue or nose. But I can smell, see, hear, and taste it all. What am I?

132. Two frogs in a bucket

Two frogs fell into a farmer's bucket of cream. One frog stopped swimming and drowned. The second frog kept kicking around and was finally able to climb out of the bucket – how?

133. Don't eat me

The poorest people have me; rich people lack me. A fool knows me, a hero fears me. If you eat me, you will die. What am I?

134. Don't leave me

The more you take, the further you go, but the more you leave me behind. What am I?

135. Letter sequence

Which letter should come next in the sequence: JFMAMJJAS

136. Hanging around for millions of years

Hanging around for millions of years, but no more than a month old – what can it be?

137. Useful to children

I start off in a mine, get taken out and enclosed in a wooden case, from which I cannot escape. No one frees me, but I am used by children around the world. What am I?

138. Used in sports

With four holes, I am used in many sports. I come in many different colors and sizes. An American state shares part of my name. What am I?

Chapter 4: Hard Riddle Answers

1. **Answer**: Why, you are, of course

2. **Answer**: In the dictionary

3. **Answer**: It's wintertime and the water was frozen

4. **Answer**: Time

5. **Answer**: He was born in room 2001 of Country Hospital

6. **Answer**: A key

7. **Answer**: Carpet

8. **Answer**: He was playing Monopoly

9. **Answer**: A watermelon

10. **Answer**: Post Office!

11. **Answer**: A piece of paper

12. **Answer**: A deck of cards

13. **Answer**: A leek

14. **Answer**: Golf

15. **Answer**: A sieve

16. **Answer**: A staircase

17. **Answer**: They're all beds

18. **Answer**: An hourglass without thousands of grains of sand

19. **Answer**: A bar of soap

20. **Answer**: Your pillow

21. **Answer**: A computer

22. **Answer**: If you spell out the numbers, they are all in alphabetical order

23. **Answer**: change the "P" in polar and make it an "S" for solar

24. **Answer**: The Amazon River was still the longest even though it had never been discovered

25. **Answer**: Polar bears since their fur is colorless. Their fur strands have a hollow core which reflects the light

26. **Answer**: Wet but it won't change colors

27. **Answer**: Microwave particles – I can cook your lunch

28. **Answer**: None, they never were alive, they are rubber ducks

29. **Answer**: Alabama, it has 3 "A"s and one "B."

30. **Answer**: Baby dolphins

31. **Answer**: A Kiwi

32. **Answer**: Castanet (cast a net)

33. **Answer**: The oldest son – how could he be mowing the yard in Boston in December?

34. **Answer**: "Are you asleep?"

35. **Answer**: Water

36. **Answer**: She lived in Australia, where it is summer during December

37. **Answer**: A toilet

38. **Answer**: A beetle

39. **Answer**: A kangaroo

40. **Answer**: A window

41. **Answer**: A waterfall

42. **Answer**: The last person takes both the basket with the last egg inside

43. **Answer**: A keyboard

44. **Answer**: A dice

45. **Answer**: A mailbox

46. **Answer**: A carrot

47. **Answer**: A secret

48. **Answer**: Glasses

49. **Answer**: It still has six legs, just because you call the antennae legs doesn't make them legs

50. **Answer**: Tuesday, Thursday, today and tomorrow

51. **Answer**: Coal (charcoal)

52. **Answer**: Banks

53. **Answer**: All of them, elephants can't jump

54. **Answer**: A hole

55. **Answer**: A tape measure

56. **Answer**: He couldn't put it down

57. **Answer**: The daughters were part of a set of quadruplets, so there were four of them

58. **Answer**: Because when you find it, you stop looking

59. **Answer**: A match

60. **Answer**: A Needle

61. **Answer**: One end of the rope was tied to the pony, but the other end wasn't tied to anything

62. **Answer**: Door #3, the lion would have died since it had nothing to eat for four months

63. **Answer**: Down at the hickory dickory dock, of course

64. **Answer**: Must have double letters

65. **Answer**: Hiss-story

66. **Answer**: A woman with a ponytail riding on the back of a horse

67. **Answer**: There are no stairs in a single-story house

68. **Answer**: He was bald

69. **Answer**: The letter "S."

70. **Answer**: The name of his horse was "Friday."

71. **Answer**: I threw it straight up in the air

72. **Answer**: Because he fell off the bottom rung

73. **Answer**: There isn't any smoke from an electric train

74. **Answer**: Only one, then it isn't an empty truck anymore

75. **Answer**: A postal carrier

76. **Answer**: French Flies

77. **Answer**: Corn on the cob

78. **Answer**: manhole covers are round so they don't fall down the hole if dropped; a square manhole cover could turn diagonally and fall down the hole

79. **Answer**: Dozens

80. **Answer**: Lightning

81. **Answer**: A puzzle piece

82. **Answer**: A glove

83. **Answer**: Neither, the yolk of an egg is always yellow

84. **Answer**: Lettuce

85. **Answer**: Really big hands

86. **Answer**: When a hot dog becomes a chili dog (hotter=spicier)

87. **Answer**: Sure, an egg won't crack a cement floor

88. **Answer**: The moon

89. **Answer**: The melon and lemon

90. **Answer**: The word "wholesome."

91. **Answer**: Bess is a horse that fell asleep outside in a field

92. **Answer**: An eye

93. **Answer**: The truck driver was walking down the road, not driving

94. **Answer**: Apple, the only one that can be eaten with its outside still on

95. **Answer**: Still the same 11 minutes, they all cook the same

96. **Answer**: A splinter in his finger

97. **Answer**: Blue =15, Yellow = 36, Red = 9

98. **Answer**: There are only three of them: grandfather, father and son (grandfather and father count as the fathers and father and son count as sons)

99. **Answer**: She was wearing her uniform

100. **Answer**: Only once. After that first subtraction, you will be subtracting from 20, then 15, then 10 (as so on)

101. **Answer**: She gets a band-aid and covers it up, no one would check to see if it really is a cut

102. **Answer**: It was a women's team playing baseball

103. **Answer**: None, crows usually fly away at the sound of gunfire

104. **Answer**: She was on a ski jump!

105. **Answer**: water (cows don't drink milk, they make milk)

106. **Answer**: He waited until winter and the lake was frozen and the man walked across the frozen lake back to safety

107. **Answer**: Mum places the sheet of newspaper until a door and closes it. Bob is on one side of the door, while Tom is one the other, but they are both on the newspaper.

108. **Answer**: Bread (did you say toast?)

109. **Answer**: Eat-Heat-Wheat

110. **Answer**: It's a coin

111. **Answer**: Pineapple

112. **Answer**: Because it's three times the money.

113. **Answer**: They are facing the interior of the ship, not the outside (sea)

114. **Answer**: sand (sandcastles; sandstorms can blind a man; sand makes glass which can be made into glasses)

115. **Answer**: It is on the outside of my shirt on the back

116. **Answer**: Gas, liquid, and solid - the states of matter

117. **Answer**: An eye

118. **Answer**: Pages 75 and 76 are opposite sides of the same page, so there couldn't be a $50 bill between them

119. **Answer**: 50% chance – there are still only two options

120. **Answer**: T-H-A-T

121. **Answer**: President Grover Cleveland was elected for two separate terms

122. **Answer**: Yes, I can – O-N-E-W-O-R-D

123. **Answer**: a jailer watches cells; a jeweler sells watches

124. **Answer**: 51 and 15

125. **Answer**: Empty

126. **Answer**: Sawdust

127. **Answer**: A white carnation

128. **Answer**: Kings out of a deck of cards

129. **Answer**: Their friend named Friday

130. **Answer**: Wrong

131. **Answer**: The human brain

132. **Answer**: All his kicking turned the cream into butter, which was solid enough for him to use to climb out

133. **Answer**: Nothing

134. **Answer**: Footsteps

135. **Answer**: O for October (initials of the months of the year)

136. **Answer**: The moon

137. **Answer**: Pencil

138. **Answer**: Jersey

Chapter 5: Difficult Riddles

"A child's mind is not a container to be filled but rather a fire to be kindled." - Dorothea Brande

1. The Walters

The Walters family live in a fancy, high-rise apartment building. They live on the 12th floor. Every morning, their daughter, Beth, leaves for school and loves riding the lift to the ground floor. But, when she comes home in the afternoon, she only rides the lift to the tenth floor and then walks up the stairs the last two floors. Why is that?

2. Mice everywhere

There are 30 mice moving around in a classroom during class, but no one is screaming. Why not?

3. Combining plus signs

How can you combine four plus signs with eight 8s to make 1000?

4. Reading in the dark

A young man is inside his apartment at night without any lights inside. He does not have a lamp, a candle, or a flashlight, yet he is still reading his favorite story. How?

5. The bus driver

You are driving a bus in Nashville. At the first stop, two teenagers get on. At the second stop, the two teenagers leave, but a woman and child get on. At the third stop, three men get on. Your bus is white and blue, and the day is full of sunshine. What color is the bus driver's hair?

6. Miles

A mother polar bear walks straight for four miles north and then three miles south. She ends up seven miles from her starting point. How is that possible?

7. Celsius vs. Fahrenheit

You are in a science class learning from Mrs. Winslow. In her experiment, she drops a ten pence piece into a glass of water that is 20 degrees Celsius and one in a glass of water that is 20 degrees Fahrenheit. Which coin sinks to the bottom faster?

8. Together on spring morning

A scarf, a carrot, and five buttons are found lying on a hill near a farmhouse. It makes total sense that they are there one spring morning. What is the reason?

9. Multiplying mice

Sam has a pair of mice in his lab. Every week, the number of mice doubles in number. Two on week one, four on week two, eight on week three, and so on. On week 10, Sam has 1,024 mice. On what week did Sam have 256 mice?

10. Verb play

Correct forms of the verb "to be" are: "I am," "He is," "You are," "She is," and "It is." But there are times you can correctly use "I is" - what are they?

11. Fire alarm

Mr. Juarez is in the middle of teaching class when the fire alarm is heard across the school. Yet, he doesn't take any of his students to any of the fire exits. Why not?

12. In alphabetical order

What number, when written out as a word, appears with each of its letters in alphabetical order?

13. Birthday cake

Maria was studying very hard for her English test. She asked her teacher, Mr. Gonzalez for help. "Which one is right: my sister chose the biggest half of my birthday cake OR my sister chose the bigger half of my birthday cake?"

14. Tree nuts

A tree grows about eight branches for every four feet of height. Each branch grew an average of two dozen nuts. How many acorns would a farmer find on a hickory tree that is 26 feet tall?

15. Not looking foolish

Mr. Edwards, my maths teacher, asked me to multiply six numbers together in front of the whole class. But I stopped listening after he said the first number. I'm sure I can still get the answer right and not look foolish - how can I be sure?

16. Farmer Brown and his haystack

Farmer Brown has a big farm. Every season he builds two haystacks in his south field and one in the north field. Every four days for the next month, Brown doubles the stacks in the south field and adds one to the north. How many bales of hay will Brown have at the end of the season if he puts them all together?

17. Surprise gift

Cindy invited 12 friends to her birthday party. They are all standing in a circle waiting to sing. Each friend can see every other friend in the room. Where can Cindy's mum put her surprise gift so everyone in the room can see it EXCEPT Cindy?

18. Farmer Bob and his animals

Farmer Bob and his wife Betty go out into their barn to check on their horses. They have three mares and a new baby colt. When they get to the barn, they find their cat, Princess, asleep in the hay. Somehow, the baby colt has escaped and is being chased by their dog, Duke. How many feet are in the barn?

19. Messy pie

Katie and Joey sneak into their mother's kitchen to eat her fresh-baked blueberry pie. Joey's face is smeared with pie, but Katie's face is clean. When they hear their mum's footsteps, Katie jumps up to clean her face while Joey sits still. Why doesn't Joey move?

20. Playing solitaire

Timmy and Tracy are in the living room playing solitaire. Timmy is behind Tracy, but Tracy is behind Timmy. How can that be?

21. Ladder in a boat

Peter's father keeps his fishing boat at the dock. The boat has a ladder that hangs over the side, almost touching the water. The rungs are 11 inches apart. How many rungs are underwater during high tide when the water raises 10 inches?

22. Closer to the US

Two cruise ships are making a journey across the Atlantic. The liner, the Meredith, leaves Great Britain on Tuesday. The second ship, the Princess, leaves the U.S. on Wednesday but has a higher speed. When they cross paths on Friday and meet in the Atlantic, which ship will be closer to the U.S.?

23. Combining water

You have two plastic jugs full of water and want to combine them in a water cooler. However, you want to be able to tell what water came from which jug. How can you put them both in the cooler and still be able to tell the water apart?

24. Science experiment

You are taking part in a science experiment. Your lab partner locks you in a basement closet where there are three light switches on the "off" position. There is one switch for each of the three bulbs on the wall inside the door. Your lab partner will only let you out of the door once, so how do you determine which switch controls which lightbulb?

Chapter 6: Difficult Riddle Answers

1. **Answer**: She is too short to reach the button for the 12th floor, so she pushes the highest number she can and then walks up the remaining floors

2. **Answer**: It is a computer class, and they are computer mice

3. **Answer**: 888+8+8++888 =1000

4. **Answer**: He is blind and reading a book in Braille

5. **Answer**: You should know your own hair color

6. **Answer**: She starts walking toward the north pole, when she reaches it, she is then walking south

7. **Answer**: 20 degrees Fahrenheit is below freezing, so the water in that glass would be ice

8. **Answer**: They were part of a snowman that melted

9. **Answer**: Week 8

10. **Answer**: "I is one of the vowels" and "I is the 9th letter is the alphabet"

11. **Answer**: He is the PE teacher and his class are outside learning to play softball, so they were already outside the building

12. **Answer**: Forty

13. **Answer**: Neither, with halves, each side are the same

14. **Answer**: None, acorns grow on Oak trees

15. **Answer**: The first number was zero - which means the answer will be 0 (zero) also

16. **Answer**: If they are all put together, there will be just one stack

17. **Answer**: Above Cindy's head

18. **Answer**: Two each for Bob and Betty - so 4 feet total (the others are paws or hooves

19. **Answer**: Katie sees the mess on Joey's face and assumes hers is just as messy. Joey sees Katie's face and assumes his is clean like hers.

20. **Answer**: none, the boat floats, so the ladder rises above the water.

21. **Answer**: they are sitting back-to-back on the floor, each playing their own game of cards

22. **Answer**: When they meet, they are both the same distance from the coast.

23. **Answer**: Freeze one of the jugs. Pour the liquid water from one jug into the cooler. Cut away the plastic jug of the other and dump the ice in. You will be able to tell them apart.

24. **Answer**: Pick one of the switches and turn it to the "on" position for 10 minutes. Then, turn that switch back to the "off" position and quickly turn the other two switches to "on," but then turn one of them back "off." Go outside the door and feel the two lights that are "off." The hottest bulb is controlled by the first switch; the other two you can tell apart as one will be "on" and one will be "off."

Did you enjoy the book?

If you did, we are ecstatic. If not, please write your complaint to us and we will make sure to fix it.

If you're feeling generous, there is something important that you can help me with – tell other people that you enjoyed the book.

Ask a grown-up to write about it on Amazon. When they do, more people will find out about the book. It also lets Amazon know that we are making kids around the world laugh. Even a few words and ratings would go a long way.

If you have any ideas or jokes that you think are super funny, please let us know. We would love to hear from you. Our email address is - **riddleland@riddlelandforkids.com**

Bonus Book!

http://bit.ly/Riddelandbonus

Thank you for buying this book. We would like to share a special bonus as a token of appreciation. It is a collection of 50 original jokes, riddles, and two funny stories.

Would you like your jokes and riddles to be featured in our next book?

We are having a contest to see who are the smartest or funniest boys and girls in the world!

1) **Creative and Challenging Riddles**
2) **Tickle Your Funny Bone Contest**

Parents, please email us your child's "Original" Riddle or Joke, **and he or she could win a $50 Amazon gift card and be featured in our next book.**

Here are the rules:
1) It must be challenging for the riddles and funny for the jokes!

2) It must be 100% Original and not something from the Internet! It is easy to find out!

3) You can submit both a joke and a riddle as they are 2 separate contests.

4) No help from the parents unless they are as funny as you.

5) Winners will be announced via email or our Facebook group – Riddleland for kids

6) Please also mention what book you purchased.

7) Email us at Riddleland@riddlelandforkids.com

Other Fun Children Books for The Kids!
Riddles Series

Try Not to Laugh Challenge Joke Series

Would You Rather Series

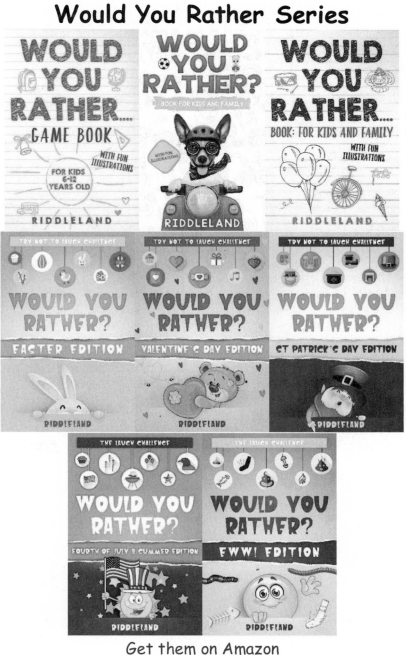

Get them on Amazon
or our website at www.riddlelandforkids.com

About Riddleland

Riddleland is a mum + dad run publishing company. We are passionate about creating fun and innovative books to help children develop their reading skills and fall in love with reading. If you have suggestions for us or want to work with us, shoot us an email at riddleland@riddlelandforkids.com

Our family's favorite quote

"Creativity is an area in which younger people have a tremendous advantage since they have an endearing habit of always questioning past wisdom and authority." – Bill Hewlett